"Reel Insights: Unveiling the Film Theories of the World"

Simranjit Singh

(Simran S Kaler)

DEDICATION

"Dedicated to the Magic of Cinema and
the Curious Minds Who Seek to Unravel
Its Secrets"

CONTENTS

1.	Formalism: Focuses on the formal elements of a film such as cinematography, editing, sound, and mise-en-scène to understand its artistic and aesthetic qualities.
2.	Realism: Emphasizes the representation of reality in films, aiming to capture the authentic human experience and social conditions.
3.	Auteur Theory: Attributes the creative vision and authorship of a film primarily to the director, considering their personal style, recurring themes, and distinct voice.
4.	Genre Theory: Examines how films fit into specific genres, identifying recurring patterns, conventions, and audience expectations associated with each genre.
5.	Semiotics: Studies the signs, symbols, and visual language used in films to understand how meaning is conveyed and interpreted.
6.	Structuralism: Analyzes the underlying structures and systems that shape the narrative, characters, and themes of a film.

7.   Psychoanalytic Theory: Draws on Freudian psychoanalysis to explore the unconscious desires, fears, and motivations of characters and viewers.

8.   Feminist Film Theory: Examines gender representation, power dynamics, and the portrayal of women in films, highlighting issues of gender inequality and stereotypes.

9.   Marxist Film Theory: Analyzes films through a Marxist lens, focusing on the portrayal of social class, economic systems, and ideologies.

10.   Postcolonial Film Theory: Investigates the representation of colonialism, imperialism, and postcolonial identities in films, challenging dominant narratives and perspectives.

11.   Queer Theory: Explores the representation of sexuality and gender identity in films, examining how films shape and challenge societal norms and constructs.

12.   Cultural Studies: Considers the social, cultural, and historical contexts in which films are produced and received, examining their impact on society and popular culture.

13.   Reception Theory: Focuses on how audiences interpret and engage with films, considering factors such as culture, ideology, and individual experiences.

14.   Cognitive Film Theory: Investigates how films engage viewers' cognitive processes, including perception, memory, attention, and emotional responses.

15.   Ecocriticism: Examines the representation of nature, environment, and ecological issues in films, exploring their socio-political and cultural implications.

16.   Social, emotional, psychological theory (SEP): Examining the level of the psychology of the viewers by constructing social structure and building an emotional spiral through the visual narrative.

ACKNOWLEDGMENTS

We would like to express our sincere gratitude to all those who contributed to the creation of this book. Without your support, expertise, and inspiration, this project would not have been possible.

We extend our deepest appreciation to the film scholars, theorists, and critics who have dedicated their lives to the study of cinema. Your groundbreaking research and insightful analyses have paved the way for this exploration into the vast world of film theories.

Our heartfelt thanks go to the filmmakers, directors, and screenwriters who have crafted masterpieces that have captivated audiences worldwide. Your visionary storytelling and artistic expressions have sparked countless discussions and interpretations.

Furthermore, we want to express our gratitude to the readers and film enthusiasts who constantly seek to expand their understanding of cinema. Your passion and curiosity fuel our collective journey into the depths of film theories.

Formalism in Film Study Theory

Formalism is a prominent film study theory that focuses on the formal elements of a film, such as cinematography, editing, sound, and mise-en-scène, to understand its artistic and aesthetic qualities. It emphasizes the technical aspects and visual language of cinema, considering how these elements contribute to the overall meaning and impact of a film. This essay will explore the key concepts and principles of formalism, its historical development, and its relevance in contemporary film analysis.

Historical Context and Development

Formalism emerged in the early 20th century, primarily in the realm of visual arts and literature. It was influenced by movements such as Russian Formalism and Structuralism, which sought to analyze and interpret artworks by focusing on their formal characteristics rather than their socio-political contexts. Formalism found its way into film theory and criticism, where scholars and theorists recognized the unique artistic potential of the medium and sought to study its specific formal elements.

Russian Formalism, led by scholars such as Viktor Shklovsky and Sergei Eisenstein, played a significant role in shaping the development of formalism in film theory. Eisenstein, in particular, introduced the concept of montage, which involves the deliberate arrangement and juxtaposition of shots to create meaning and evoke emotions. Eisenstein's films, like "Battleship Potemkin" (1925), exemplified the power of editing and montage to convey political messages and elicit a visceral response from the audience.

Key Concepts and Principles

1. Cinematography: Formalism places a strong emphasis on the visual composition and camera work in a film. It considers how camera angles, movements, framing, lighting, and color contribute to the narrative, mood, and overall aesthetic appeal. Cinematography can create symbolism, evoke emotions, and guide the viewer's attention to specific elements within the frame.

2.	Editing: Editing is a crucial element in formalist analysis. It explores the arrangement of shots, transitions, and pacing to create meaning and impact. Formalist theorists analyze the rhythm, continuity, or disruption of editing techniques to understand how they shape the viewer's perception and interpretation of the film. Montage, as mentioned earlier, is a key editing concept within formalism.

3.	Sound: Formalism acknowledges the importance of sound in film as a formal element. It considers how dialogue, music, sound effects, and silence contribute to the narrative, atmosphere, and emotional engagement. Formalist analysis examines the relationship between sound and image, looking at the ways in which sound enhances or contrasts with the visual elements.

4.	Mise-en-scène: Mise-en-scène refers to the arrangement of elements within a shot, including sets, costumes, props, and the positioning and movement of characters. Formalism examines how the visual elements within a frame work together to convey meaning and contribute to the overall aesthetic appeal of a film. It considers the composition, symmetry, and visual patterns within the frame.

5.   Formal Patterns and Structures: Formalism seeks to identify recurring patterns, structures, and motifs within a film that contribute to its overall coherence and artistic merit. It explores the repetition of visual and auditory elements, narrative devices, and stylistic choices that create unity and convey a particular vision.

6.   Artistic Intention: Formalism acknowledges the role of the filmmaker's artistic intention in shaping the formal elements of a film. It considers how the director's choices in cinematography, editing, sound, and mise-en-scène reflect their creative vision and contribute to the overall meaning and impact of the film.

Relevance and Contemporary Application

Formalism continues to be relevant in contemporary film analysis and criticism. Its emphasis on the technical and aesthetic aspects of cinema allows for a close examination of the craft and artistry involved in filmmaking. By analyzing the formal elements, scholars and theorists can uncover the nuances, symbolism, and thematic depth embedded within a film.

Formalist analysis can provide insights into the visual storytelling techniques employed by filmmakers and how they shape the viewer's perception and emotional engagement. By studying the composition, camera movements, and editing choices, analysts can decode the director's intentions and the intended impact on the audience.

Additionally, formalism complements other film study theories and approaches. It can be integrated with theories such as psychoanalysis, feminism, or postcolonialism to explore how formal elements contribute to the representation of psychological states, gender dynamics, or cultural contexts within a film. By considering both the formal and thematic dimensions, a more comprehensive understanding of a film can be achieved.

Formalism is not without its criticisms, however. Some argue that a sole focus on formal elements may overlook the socio-political and cultural contexts in which films are made and received. Critics argue that ignoring the content and subtext of a film in favor of formal analysis can limit the understanding of its broader implications.

In conclusion, formalism is a valuable film study theory that highlights the significance of formal elements in understanding the artistic and aesthetic qualities of a film. By analyzing cinematography, editing, sound, and mise-en-scène, formalism provides a framework for appreciating the technical craftsmanship and visual language of cinema. Its historical development, key concepts, and principles offer valuable tools for analyzing films, and its integration with other theories can lead to a more comprehensive understanding of cinematic works.

Realism in Film Study Theory

Realism is a significant film study theory that focuses on the representation of reality in films. It seeks to capture the authentic human experience and social conditions, portraying characters and narratives that resonate with the viewers' lived realities. This essay will explore the key concepts and principles of realism, its historical development, and its relevance in contemporary film analysis.

Historical Context and Development

Realism as a film theory has its roots in literary and artistic movements that emerged in the late 19th and early 20th centuries. It was a response to the prevailing romanticism and idealism of the time, which often depicted fantastical or exaggerated representations of life. Realism sought to present a more truthful and objective portrayal of the world, reflecting the social, political, and economic realities of the time.

In film, realism gained prominence during the Italian Neorealism movement in the 1940s and 1950s. Filmmakers like Roberto Rossellini, Vittorio De Sica, and Luchino Visconti created films that depicted the struggles of ordinary people in post-World War II Italy. These films often featured non-professional actors, real locations, and stories inspired by actual events, aiming to provide an unfiltered view of society and its problems.

Key Concepts and Principles

1. Authenticity and Verisimilitude: Realism emphasizes the portrayal of reality as accurately and truthfully as possible. It seeks to create an illusion of reality on screen by using naturalistic settings, believable dialogue, and performances that feel genuine. Realist films often avoid excessive stylization or manipulation, aiming to capture the nuances and complexities of human behavior and social interactions.

2. Social Commentary: Realism often incorporates social commentary,

addressing social issues, inequalities, and power dynamics. By presenting stories and characters rooted in real-world contexts, realist films can shed light on the struggles and challenges faced by individuals and communities. They provide a platform for critical examination and reflection on society's structures and values.

3. Everyday Life: Realism is concerned with depicting the everyday experiences and routines of ordinary people. It focuses on mundane activities, domestic spaces, and the struggles and aspirations of individuals from various social backgrounds. Realist films often highlight the significance of the seemingly ordinary, allowing viewers to connect with the characters and their situations.

4. Location and Environment: Realism emphasizes the use of authentic locations and environments to enhance the sense of realism. Filming in real settings, rather than constructed sets, adds a level of authenticity and immersion for the audience. Realist filmmakers often choose to shoot on location, capturing the unique

characteristics and atmosphere of a particular place.

5.   Non-Professional Actors: Realism often utilizes non-professional actors or actors who have a close connection to the characters they portray. This approach adds an additional layer of authenticity, as the performers bring their own lived experiences and perspectives to the roles. The use of non-professional actors can blur the lines between fiction and reality, further enhancing the sense of realism.

6.   Cinematic Style: Realism typically employs a straightforward and unobtrusive cinematic style. It avoids excessive stylization, flashy editing techniques, or artificial embellishments. Realist films often feature long takes, minimalistic camera movements, and natural lighting to maintain a sense of observational detachment and authenticity.

Relevance and Contemporary Application

Realism continues to be a relevant and influential film study theory in contemporary cinema. Filmmakers and audiences value realism for its ability to depict relatable and socially relevant stories. Realist films can provide a powerful critique of societal norms, challenge dominant ideologies, and provoke empathy and understanding.

Contemporary filmmakers often draw from the principles of realism while exploring new storytelling techniques and narrative structures. They may combine elements of realism with other stylistic approaches or genres to create innovative and thought-provoking works. Realism remains a foundation that allows filmmakers to engage with pressing social issues and reflect the complexities of the human experience.

Realism is not without its criticisms. Some argue that an exclusive focus on realism may limit artistic freedom and overlook the subjective and imaginative aspects of filmmaking. Critics suggest that a purely realist approach may neglect the potential of cinema as a medium for artistic expression, symbolism, and allegory.

In conclusion, realism is a significant film study theory that emphasizes the authentic representation of reality in films. Its historical development, key concepts, and principles provide a framework for understanding how filmmakers capture the complexities of the human experience and social conditions. Realism continues to be relevant in contemporary cinema, as it allows for critical examination of societal issues and resonates with audiences seeking relatable and thought-provoking narratives.

Auteur Theory in Film Study

Auteur theory is a prominent film study theory that attributes the creative vision and authorship of a film primarily to the director. It emphasizes the director's role as the primary artist and auteur, shaping the film's artistic and thematic elements. Auteur theory considers a director's unique style, recurring themes, and distinct voice as essential factors in analysing and interpreting films. This essay will delve into the key concepts and principles of auteur theory, its historical development, and its relevance in contemporary film analysis.

Historical Context and Development

Auteur theory emerged in the 1950s and 1960s, primarily in French film criticism circles associated with the journal Cahiers du Cinéma. It was championed by critics such as François Truffaut, Jean-Luc Godard, and Eric Rohmer. These critics believed that cinema should be regarded as an art form, and directors should be recognized as the primary creative force behind films.

The proponents of auteur theory drew inspiration from earlier movements, such as the French New Wave, which celebrated directors' personal style, experimentation, and authorial control. They rejected the prevailing notion that films were solely a commercial product or collaborative effort, instead elevating the director to the status of an artist with a distinctive artistic vision.

Key Concepts and Principles

1.   Director as the Author: Auteur theory considers the director as the primary author of a film, akin to a writer's role in literature or a painter's role in visual arts. It asserts that the director's creative decisions and personal vision are the driving forces behind a film's artistic and thematic qualities. The director's style, choices in cinematography, editing, storytelling, and use of recurring themes are seen as distinguishing marks of their authorship.

2.   Signature Style: Auteur theory emphasizes a director's unique style and recurring thematic preoccupations as significant elements of their authorship. A director's signature style may manifest through visual choices, such as

cinematography, mise-en-scène, and use of camera movement, as well as narrative techniques, editing strategies, and the treatment of characters and themes. These distinct characteristics are seen as the director's artistic imprint on the film.

3. Intertextuality and Continuity: Auteur theory considers a director's body of work as a coherent and interconnected body of artistic expression. It looks for intertextual references, recurring motifs, visual and thematic consistency, and a sense of continuity across the director's films. This approach allows for a deeper understanding of the director's artistic development, evolution, and exploration of specific themes or ideas throughout their filmography.

4. Personal Vision and Control: Auteur theory values a director's creative control and the realization of their personal vision. It emphasizes the director's role in guiding the film's artistic decisions, from script development to post-production. Auteurist analysis often explores how a director's vision influences the film's

formal elements, narrative structure, character development, and overall meaning.

5. Evaluation of Directorial Body of Work: Auteur theory considers a director's entire body of work when evaluating their artistic merit and significance. It encourages the examination of stylistic consistency, thematic exploration, and evolution of the director's ideas across multiple films. Auteurist analysis often seeks to identify the director's strengths, recurring themes, and the ways in which they contribute to the medium of cinema.

Relevance and Contemporary Application

Auteur theory remains relevant and influential in contemporary film analysis and criticism. It offers a framework for understanding and appreciating a director's artistic vision, allowing for a deeper exploration of their body of work. Auteurist analysis enables scholars and critics to examine how a director's choices and personal style contribute to the film's overall impact, thematic depth, and artistic integrity.

Genre Theory in Film Study

Genre theory is a fundamental and influential approach in film study that examines how films are categorized into distinct genres based on their narrative, themes, and stylistic conventions. It explores the patterns, conventions, and expectations associated with different genres, allowing for a deeper understanding of how films communicate meaning, engage audiences, and participate in cultural discourse. This essay will delve into the key concepts and principles of genre theory, its historical development, and its relevance in contemporary film analysis.

Historical Context and Development

Genre theory has its roots in literary studies, where the concept of genre has long been used to classify and analyze different forms of literature. In the early 20th century, genre theory was adapted to the study of film, with early scholars such as André Bazin and Jean Mitry examining the patterns and conventions that distinguished various types of films. The development of genre theory gained further momentum in the 1960s and 1970s with the work of film theorists and scholars such as Rick Altman, Steve Neale, and Thomas Schatz. These scholars explored the cultural, social, and industrial aspects of genres, delving into how genres are created, evolve over time, and interact with audience expectations and reception.

Key Concepts and Principles

1. Classification and Typology: Genre theory involves the classification and categorization of films into specific genres. Genres are defined by shared narrative structures, themes, stylistic elements, and audience expectations. Genres provide a framework for understanding and analyzing films based on their formal and thematic characteristics.

2. Conventions and Patterns: Each genre has its own set of conventions, patterns, and tropes that define its identity and distinguish it from other genres. These conventions include

narrative structures, character types, visual styles, settings, and thematic motifs. Genre theory explores how these conventions are employed and subverted within individual films, contributing to audience engagement and the creation of meaning.

3. Audience Expectations: Genre theory recognizes the role of audience expectations in shaping the reception and interpretation of films. Audiences develop a set of expectations based on their familiarity with specific genres, and filmmakers often cater to these expectations to engage and satisfy viewers. Genre films often fulfill and challenge audience expectations, creating a dynamic interaction between filmmakers and their audiences.

4. Genre Evolution and Hybridity: Genres are not static entities but evolve and adapt over time. Genre theory acknowledges the historical development and transformation of genres, as well as the emergence of hybrid genres that combine elements from multiple genres. Films can experiment with genre boundaries, blending or subverting conventions to

create innovative and unique storytelling experiences.

5. Cultural and Social Significance: Genres are not just aesthetic categories but also reflect and participate in cultural and social discourse. Genre theory examines how genres intersect with cultural values, ideologies, and historical contexts. Genres can address social issues, reflect cultural anxieties, or provide commentary on contemporary events, making them significant cultural artifacts.

6. Genre and Industry: Genre theory acknowledges the industrial aspects of filmmaking and how genres serve commercial purposes within the film industry. Studios and distributors use genre classifications to market films, target specific audiences, and capitalize on established audience preferences. Genre theory explores the relationship between genre conventions, audience reception, and the economic aspects of film production and distribution.

Relevance and Contemporary Application

Genre theory continues to be a relevant and influential approach in contemporary film analysis and criticism. It offers a framework for understanding the ways in which films communicate, engage, and participate in cultural and social discourses. Genre analysis allows scholars and critics to examine the conventions, patterns, and audience expectations associated with specific genres, offering insights into how films create meaning, evoke emotions, and reflect societal concerns. Contemporary filmmakers often draw from genre conventions while subverting or reinterpreting them to create innovative and thought-provoking works. They may combine elements from multiple genres, experiment with genre boundaries, or create new hybrid genres that challenge traditional classifications. Genre theory provides a foundation for examining these creative endeavors and understanding the ways in which filmmakers engage with and push the boundaries of established genres.

In conclusion, genre theory is a significant and influential approach in film study that examines the classification, conventions, and audience expectations associated with different genres. It offers a framework for understanding how genres shape the formal and thematic elements of films, as well as their cultural and social significance. Genre theory allows for a deeper analysis of films, enabling scholars and critics to explore how genres communicate meaning, engage audiences, and reflect the complexities of the human experience.

Semiotics Theory in Film Study

Semiotics theory is a critical framework that explores the study of signs, symbols, and meaning-making processes within film. It focuses on understanding how films communicate and convey messages through the use of visual, auditory, and narrative elements. By analyzing the signs and codes employed in films, semiotics theory provides insights into the cultural, social, and ideological dimensions of cinema. This essay will delve into the key concepts and principles of semiotics theory, its historical development, and its relevance in contemporary film analysis.

Historical Context and Development

Semiotics, or the study of signs and symbols, has its origins in the work of Swiss linguist Ferdinand de Saussure and American philosopher Charles Sanders

Peirce in the late 19th and early 20th centuries. Saussure proposed a structuralist approach to language, arguing that meaning is derived from the relationship between signs, signifiers (the physical form of a sign), and signifieds (the mental concept or idea associated with a sign). Peirce, on the other hand, developed a broader theory of signs, encompassing not only language but also visual and cultural signs.

In the context of film studies, semiotics theory gained prominence in the 1960s and 1970s with the work of scholars such as Christian Metz, Umberto Eco, and Roland Barthes. These theorists applied semiotic principles to analyze the visual, narrative, and symbolic elements in films, shedding light on how meaning is constructed and communicated within the cinematic medium.

Key Concepts and Principles

1.   Sign and Signifier: In semiotics theory, a sign is a unit of meaning composed of a signifier (the form or physical manifestation of the sign) and a signified (the concept or meaning

associated with the sign). In film, signs can be visual (such as images, colors, or gestures), auditory (such as music or dialogue), or narrative (such as plot structures or character archetypes). The relationship between the signifier and the signified is not fixed but is shaped by cultural and social contexts.

2. Codes and Conventions: Semiotics theory explores the use of codes and conventions in film, which are systems of shared meanings and rules that enable communication. Codes can be cultural, where meanings are shaped by societal norms and values, or cinematic, where meanings are derived from established film conventions and genres. By analyzing codes and conventions, semiotic analysis can uncover the ways in which films convey specific messages and engage with audiences.

3. Icon, Index, and Symbol: Semiotics theory distinguishes between different types of signs. Icons are signs that have a physical resemblance or similarity to their referents (e.g., a photograph). Indexes are signs that have a direct causal or associative

relationship with their referents (e.g., smoke as a sign of fire). Symbols, on the other hand, are signs that are culturally constructed and have arbitrary relationships with their referents (e.g., a national flag). Understanding these different types of signs can reveal the layers of meaning embedded within a film.

4. Semiotic Analysis: Semiotic analysis involves the examination of signs, codes, and conventions within a film to uncover the underlying meanings and messages being communicated. This analysis can focus on various levels, including individual signs, narrative structures, visual motifs, and cultural contexts. By deconstructing the elements of a film and their relationships, semiotics theory helps elucidate the ways in which films construct and convey meaning.

5. Cultural and Ideological Analysis: Semiotics theory acknowledges the cultural and ideological dimensions of signs and symbols. Films are not created in a vacuum but are influenced by the cultural and social contexts in which they are produced and received.

Semiotic analysis can uncover the ways in which films reflect and perpetuate dominant ideologies, challenge societal norms, or reinforce cultural stereotypes. By examining the cultural implications of signs and symbols in film, semiotics theory allows for a critical understanding of the power dynamics and ideological influences at play.

Relevance and Contemporary Application

Semiotics theory continues to be a valuable and relevant approach in contemporary film analysis and criticism. It provides a framework for understanding how films communicate meaning through signs, symbols, and codes. Semiotic analysis allows scholars and critics to unpack the layers of meaning within a film, uncover hidden messages, and examine the cultural and ideological implications of cinematic representations.

Contemporary filmmakers often draw on semiotic principles to create films that engage audiences on multiple levels and convey complex narratives. They employ visual and auditory elements strategically to evoke emotions, convey themes, and communicate ideas. Semiotic analysis enables a deeper understanding of the formal and thematic choices made by filmmakers and offers insights into how audiences interpret and engage with films.

Moreover, in an era of media convergence and digital technologies, semiotics theory can be applied to analyze a wide range of audiovisual media beyond traditional cinema. From television shows to advertisements, music videos to online content, semiotics provides a versatile framework for understanding the intricate ways in which signs and symbols shape our understanding of visual culture.

In conclusion, semiotics theory offers a rich and nuanced approach to film study by examining the signs, symbols, and meaning-making processes within films. By analyzing the relationships between signs and their cultural and social contexts, semiotic analysis allows for a deeper understanding of how films communicate and engage with audiences. Semiotics theory remains relevant in contemporary film analysis, empowering scholars and critics to unravel the layers of meaning embedded within cinematic texts and explore the cultural, social, and ideological dimensions of cinema.

Structuralism Theory in Film Study

Structuralism theory is a foundational framework in film study that focuses on the underlying structures, patterns, and systems of meaning within films. It examines the relationships between different elements and analyzes how these elements work together to create meaning. By exploring the formal and narrative structures of films, structuralism theory provides insights into the ways in which films convey messages, construct representations, and engage with audiences. This essay will delve into the key concepts and principles of structuralism theory, its

historical development, and its relevance in contemporary film analysis.
Historical Context and Development
Structuralism emerged as a theoretical approach in the fields of linguistics and anthropology in the early 20th century. It gained prominence in the 1960s and 1970s, extending its influence to various disciplines, including film studies. Structuralist film theory sought to understand films as systems of signs and signifiers, emphasizing the relationships between these signs and the underlying structures that govern their meaning.
Key Concepts and Principles
1. Structures and Systems: Structuralism theory views films as structures composed of various elements, including images, sounds, narrative patterns, and symbolic representations. These elements form interconnected systems that contribute to the overall meaning of the film. Structuralist analysis examines the ways in which these elements are organized and interconnected, uncovering the underlying structures that shape the film's form and content.

2.	Binary Oppositions: Structuralism theory emphasizes the presence of binary oppositions within films, wherein two contrasting elements are positioned against each other. These oppositions can exist at various levels, such as character relationships, thematic motifs, or visual representations. Structuralist analysis explores how these oppositions create tension, conflict, and meaning within the film, reflecting broader cultural or social dichotomies.

3.	Structuralist Narratology: Structuralism theory examines the narrative structures of films, focusing on the organization of plot, character development, and temporal sequencing. It explores the ways in which films establish narrative coherence, causality, and progression. Structuralist analysis may involve identifying narrative patterns, recurring motifs, and archetypal characters to uncover the underlying structures that shape the film's storytelling.

4.	Signification and Meaning: Structuralism theory explores how films create meaning through signification. It emphasizes that meaning is not inherent in the individual elements of a film but arises from their relationships within the overall structure. Structuralist analysis examines the ways in which signs and signifiers interact, producing layers of meaning that are contingent on cultural and social contexts.

5.   Intertextuality and Intercodality: Structuralism theory recognizes the intertextual and intercodal relationships within films. Intertextuality refers to the references, allusions, or borrowing of elements from other texts, such as literature or previous films, within a film. Intercodality involves the interaction of different systems of signs, such as visual, auditory, and linguistic codes, within a film. Structuralist analysis explores how these intertextual and intercodal relationships contribute to the film's overall meaning and shape its cultural and aesthetic significance.

Relevance and Contemporary Application

Structuralism theory continues to be relevant and influential in contemporary film analysis and criticism. It offers a systematic framework for understanding the underlying structures and patterns that shape the form and meaning of films. Structuralist analysis enables scholars and critics to uncover the complex relationships between different elements within films, shedding light on how meaning is constructed and conveyed to audiences.

Contemporary filmmakers often draw from structuralist principles to create films that engage audiences through intricate narrative structures, visual compositions, and symbolic representations. They employ formal and narrative strategies to construct meaning, create resonance, and challenge traditional storytelling conventions. Structuralist analysis allows for a deeper understanding of these creative choices and offers insights into the ways in which filmmakers navigate the complex web of structures and systems within their films.

Moreover, structuralism theory's influence extends beyond film analysis to other forms of visual media, including television shows, advertising, and digital content. Its emphasis on structures, systems, and intertextual relationships provides a valuable lens for examining the complexities of visual culture and the ways in which meaning is constructed within various media forms. In conclusion, structuralism theory offers a comprehensive framework for analyzing the underlying structures, patterns, and systems of meaning within films. By exploring the relationships between different elements and examining the formal and narrative structures of films, structuralist analysis allows for a deeper understanding of how films communicate, construct representations, and engage with audiences. Structuralism theory remains relevant in contemporary film analysis, empowering scholars and critics to unravel the layers of meaning embedded within cinematic texts and explore the intricacies of visual storytelling.

Psychoanalytic Theory in Film Study

Psychoanalytic theory is a psychological framework that has been widely applied in film studies to analyze the unconscious motivations, desires, and conflicts portrayed within films. Developed by Sigmund Freud in the late 19th and early 20th centuries, psychoanalysis explores the complex interplay between the conscious and unconscious mind. When applied to film analysis, psychoanalytic theory allows for an in-depth examination of characters, narratives, and themes, shedding light on the psychological dimensions of cinematic storytelling.

This essay will delve into the key concepts and principles of psychoanalytic theory, its historical development, and its relevance in contemporary film analysis.

Historical Context and Development

Psychoanalytic theory was formulated by Sigmund Freud, an Austrian neurologist and psychoanalyst, in the late 19th and early 20th centuries. Freud's groundbreaking work introduced concepts such as the unconscious, dreams, repression, and the Oedipus complex. These concepts explored the hidden motivations, desires, and conflicts that shape human behavior. Over time, psychoanalytic theory evolved and diversified, with different schools of thought emerging, including Freudian, Jungian, and Lacanian psychoanalysis.

Psychoanalytic theory's application to film studies gained momentum in the mid-20th century with the work of film theorists such as Hugo Münsterberg and Christian Metz. They sought to understand the ways in which films tapped into the unconscious desires and fantasies of audiences, as well as the ways in which filmmakers expressed their own psychological insights and concerns through their work.

Key Concepts and Principles

1. Unconscious Mind: Psychoanalytic theory emphasizes the importance of the unconscious mind, which comprises thoughts, desires, and memories that are not readily accessible to conscious awareness. It suggests that unconscious processes heavily influence human behavior, including the creation and reception of films. Psychoanalytic film analysis aims to uncover the unconscious motivations and desires embedded within films and the ways in which they resonate with viewers.

2. Dreams and Symbols: Psychoanalysis places significance on dreams and the symbolic language used by the unconscious to express hidden desires and conflicts. Similarly, films often employ symbolism and dream-like sequences to convey psychological states and explore unconscious themes. Psychoanalytic analysis looks for recurring symbols, metaphors, and dream imagery within films to

understand their psychological implications.

3. Oedipus Complex and Family Dynamics: The Oedipus complex, a central concept in psychoanalytic theory, refers to the unconscious desire of a child for the parent of the opposite sex and rivalry with the same-sex parent. Psychoanalytic film analysis examines the portrayal of family dynamics, particularly the relationships between parents and children, to uncover unconscious desires, conflicts, and power dynamics.

4. Defense Mechanisms and Repression: Psychoanalytic theory posits that individuals employ defense mechanisms, such as repression, to protect themselves from unconscious desires and conflicts that may cause anxiety. In films, characters often exhibit various defense mechanisms, which can be analyzed to understand their psychological struggles and internal conflicts. Repressed memories and desires can manifest symbolically or erupt into conscious awareness, driving the narrative forward.

5. Catharsis and Sublimation: Psychoanalysis recognizes the cathartic potential of art, including film, as a means for individuals to safely explore and release repressed emotions and desires. Films can provide a space for viewers to vicariously experience and process their own unconscious fears, desires, and anxieties. Psychoanalytic film analysis examines the emotional and psychological impact of films, exploring how they can evoke catharsis or sublimate unconscious desires through aesthetic and narrative choices.

6. Transference and Identification: Psychoanalytic theory emphasizes the concepts of transference and identification. Transference refers to the projection of unresolved conflicts and desires onto fictional characters, while identification involves the viewer emotionally aligning themselves with the experiences and perspectives of characters. Psychoanalytic analysis examines the ways in which viewers project their own unconscious desires, conflicts, and fantasies onto film characters and narratives.

Relevance and Contemporary Application

Psychoanalytic theory remains a relevant and influential approach in contemporary film analysis and criticism. It provides a unique perspective on the psychological dimensions of cinematic storytelling, allowing for a deeper understanding of character motivations, narrative structures, and thematic resonances. Psychoanalytic analysis enables scholars and critics to uncover the unconscious layers of meaning within films and explore the ways in which they engage with viewers on a psychological level.

Contemporary filmmakers often draw on psychoanalytic principles to create films that explore complex human experiences, delve into the depths of the unconscious, and challenge societal norms. They employ symbolic imagery, dream sequences, and narrative devices to evoke psychological responses and provoke introspection. Psychoanalytic analysis enables a deeper understanding of these creative choices and offers insights into the psychological impact and cultural significance of films.

Moreover, psychoanalytic theory's influence extends beyond traditional cinema to other forms of visual media, including television shows, advertising, and digital content. Its focus on unconscious motivations, desires, and conflicts provides a valuable framework for understanding the complexities of human psychology and the ways in which visual media can tap into and shape collective unconscious experiences.

In conclusion, psychoanalytic theory offers a rich and insightful approach to film study by exploring the unconscious motivations, desires, and conflicts embedded within films. By analyzing characters, narratives, and symbolic imagery, psychoanalytic analysis allows for a deeper understanding of the psychological dimensions of cinematic storytelling. Psychoanalytic theory remains relevant in contemporary film analysis, empowering scholars and critics to unravel the layers of unconscious meaning within films and explore the intricate ways in which they engage with viewers on a psychological level.

Feminist Film Theory in Film Study

Feminist film theory is a critical framework that examines the representation of women in film, explores gender dynamics, and challenges patriarchal ideologies and norms within cinematic narratives. It emerged in the 1960s and 1970s as part of the larger feminist movement and has since evolved to encompass a diverse range of perspectives and approaches.

Feminist film theory seeks to analyze the ways in which films perpetuate or subvert gender stereotypes, address issues of female agency and subjectivity, and promote gender equality. This essay will delve into the key concepts and principles of feminist film theory, its historical development, and its relevance in contemporary film analysis.

Historical Context and Development

Feminist film theory emerged in the context of the women's liberation movement of the 1960s and 1970s. It aimed to challenge the predominantly male-dominated film industry, critique the representation of women on screen, and advocate for greater visibility and agency for women both behind and in front of the camera. Feminist scholars and activists analyzed films through a feminist lens, identifying patriarchal structures, gender biases, and stereotypes prevalent in mainstream cinema.

Key Concepts and Principles

1.   Gender Representation: Feminist film theory focuses on the representation of gender in films and examines how women are portrayed on

screen. It analyzes the ways in which films construct and perpetuate gender stereotypes, objectification, and the male gaze. Feminist scholars emphasize the need for diverse and authentic representations of women, challenging traditional tropes and narratives that limit women's agency and reinforce patriarchal ideologies.

2.   Intersectionality: Feminist film theory recognizes that gender cannot be analyzed in isolation but intersects with other aspects of identity, such as race, class, sexuality, and ethnicity. Intersectionality highlights the different experiences and struggles of women from diverse backgrounds and examines how these intersecting identities shape their representation in film. It calls for an inclusive and intersectional approach to feminist film analysis that accounts for multiple layers of oppression and privilege.

3.   Female Authorship: Feminist film theory emphasizes the importance of female filmmakers, writers, and directors in challenging patriarchal norms and providing alternative narratives. It recognizes the significance

of women's perspectives and experiences in shaping the cinematic landscape. Feminist analysis considers the role of women behind the camera, exploring how their presence influences storytelling, representation, and the overall aesthetics of films.

4.   The Male Gaze: The concept of the male gaze, coined by feminist film theorist Laura Mulvey, highlights the ways in which the camera and narrative are structured to align with a heterosexual male perspective. It reflects the objectification and sexualization of women on screen, positioning them as passive objects of desire. Feminist film theory critiques and subverts the male gaze, seeking to challenge and disrupt traditional power dynamics and create space for alternative narratives and perspectives.

5.   Feminist Narratives and Storytelling: Feminist film theory advocates for the inclusion of feminist narratives and storytelling techniques that center women's experiences, voices, and struggles. It explores how films can challenge traditional narrative structures, disrupt gender norms, and

promote narratives that empower and validate women's perspectives. Feminist analysis looks for narratives that resist patriarchal conventions and provide nuanced portrayals of women's lives and identities.

Relevance and Contemporary Application

Feminist film theory remains relevant and influential in contemporary film analysis and criticism. It offers a critical lens through which scholars and critics can examine the representation of gender in films and uncover the ways in which patriarchal ideologies are embedded within cinematic narratives. Feminist analysis enables a deeper understanding of how films reflect and shape societal attitudes towards gender, power, and equality.

Contemporary filmmakers increasingly incorporate feminist perspectives and principles into their work, aiming to challenge gender norms and amplify women's voices. They create films that explore diverse female experiences, address intersectional identities, and challenge the status quo. Feminist film analysis allows for a comprehensive examination of these creative choices, highlighting the ways in which filmmakers contribute to the feminist discourse and promote social change through their storytelling.

Feminist film theory also extends its influence beyond traditional cinema to other forms of visual media, including television shows, web series, and digital content. It provides a framework for analyzing the representation of gender in a wide range of visual narratives, exploring how they contribute to broader discussions on feminism, gender equality, and social justice.

In conclusion, feminist film theory offers a critical framework for analyzing the representation of gender in films, challenging patriarchal ideologies, and advocating for greater equality and visibility for women in cinema. By examining gender representation, intersectionality, female authorship, the male gaze, and feminist narratives, feminist film analysis provides valuable insights into the ways in which films reflect and shape societal attitudes towards gender and power dynamics. Feminist film theory remains relevant in contemporary film analysis, empowering scholars and critics to engage with films through a feminist lens and promote inclusive and empowering narratives within the cinematic landscape.

Marxist Film Theory in Film Study

Marxist film theory is a critical framework that analyzes films through the lens of Marxist theory, examining how they reflect and perpetuate class struggle, economic inequality, and capitalist ideologies. Developed from the writings of Karl Marx and Friedrich Engels, Marxist theory explores the relationships between social classes and the economic systems that shape society. Marxist film theory seeks to uncover the ways in which films portray and reinforce class divisions, critique capitalist structures, and provide a platform for social critique. This essay will delve into the key concepts and principles of Marxist film theory, its historical development, and its relevance in contemporary film analysis.

Historical Context and Development

Marxist film theory emerged in the early 20th century, parallel to the rise of Marxism as a powerful critique of capitalist societies. Early Marxist theorists, such as Georg Lukács and Bertolt Brecht, sought to understand the ways in which art and culture intersected with economic systems. They argued that films, as a popular form of entertainment and cultural expression, played a significant role in shaping and reflecting class consciousness.

Key Concepts and Principles

1.   Class Struggle: Central to Marxist film theory is the concept of class struggle, which refers to the conflict between the working class (proletariat)

and the owning class (bourgeoisie). Marxist analysis examines how films depict and perpetuate this class struggle, either by reinforcing capitalist ideologies or by presenting narratives that challenge and critique the existing social and economic order.

2.   Economic Determinism: Marxist theory posits that economic systems shape the social and cultural dynamics of a society. In the context of film, Marxist analysis explores how economic relations and structures are reflected in the narratives, characters, and themes depicted on screen. It investigates the ways in which films portray and critique capitalist ideologies and the unequal distribution of wealth and resources.

3.   Ideological Critique: Marxist film theory engages in ideological critique, examining how films reflect and promote dominant ideologies and values. It investigates how the ruling class uses cultural production, including films, to shape public opinion, maintain social order, and perpetuate the status quo. Marxist analysis seeks to uncover hidden messages, ideological biases, and the ways in which films either challenge

or reinforce the dominant capitalist ideology.

4. Modes of Production: Marxist analysis pays attention to the modes of production depicted in films, including the labor process and the economic relations between characters. It examines how films portray issues such as exploitation, alienation, and commodification of labor, shedding light on the underlying economic dynamics and power imbalances within cinematic narratives.

5. Historical Materialism: Marxist film theory employs the concept of historical materialism, which explores the relationship between historical developments and the economic base of society. It analyzes how films reflect the social and historical contexts in which they are produced, exploring the ways in which specific historical moments influence the portrayal of class relations and capitalist structures.

Relevance and Contemporary Application

Marxist film theory remains a relevant and influential approach in contemporary film analysis and criticism. It provides a critical framework for understanding the ways in which films reflect and perpetuate social inequalities, class divisions, and capitalist ideologies. Marxist analysis allows scholars and critics to engage with films as cultural products that both shape and are shaped by economic systems and power structures.

Contemporary filmmakers often draw on Marxist principles to create films that critique capitalist structures, address social injustices, and provide alternative narratives. They explore themes of economic inequality, labor exploitation, and resistance to capitalist ideologies. Marxist film analysis enables a deeper understanding of these creative choices, highlighting the ways in which filmmakers contribute to social critique and political consciousness through their storytelling.

Moreover, Marxist film theory's influence extends beyond traditional cinema to other forms of visual media, including documentaries, television shows, and digital content. It provides a framework for analyzing the representation of class

Postcolonial Film Theory in Film Study

Postcolonial film theory is a critical framework that examines the representation of colonial and postcolonial experiences in films, explores power dynamics, cultural identity, and challenges colonial ideologies and discourses within cinematic narratives. It emerged in the late 20th century as part of the larger postcolonial movement, which sought to critique and subvert the legacies of colonialism and imperialism. Postcolonial film theory aims to analyze the ways in which films reflect and engage with the complexities of colonial histories, decolonization, and the ongoing struggles for cultural, social, and political liberation. This essay will delve into the key concepts and principles of postcolonial film theory, its historical development, and its relevance in contemporary film analysis.

Historical Context and Development

Postcolonial film theory emerged in the wake of global decolonization movements and the growing recognition of the need to critically engage with the legacies of colonialism. It draws from postcolonial studies, which emerged in the 1970s and 1980s, and examines the intersections of race, culture, and power in the aftermath of colonial rule. Postcolonial film theorists analyze films through a postcolonial lens, identifying and critiquing the ways in which films reflect and perpetuate colonial ideologies, stereotypes, and power dynamics.

Key Concepts and Principles

1. Colonialism and Imperialism: Postcolonial film theory engages with the historical contexts of colonialism and imperialism, exploring how these systems of domination shape the narratives, characters, and themes depicted in films. It examines how films represent colonial encounters, the effects of colonization on colonized peoples, and the struggles for independence and decolonization. Postcolonial analysis seeks to challenge and subvert the colonial gaze and narratives that reinforce colonial power structures.

2. Cultural Identity and Representation: Postcolonial film theory emphasizes the representation of cultural identities within films. It examines how films portray the complexities of postcolonial identities, diasporic experiences, and the negotiation of hybrid and liminal identities. Postcolonial analysis explores the ways in which films challenge essentialist notions of identity and offer nuanced portrayals of diverse cultural perspectives.

3. Subaltern Voices and Counter-Narratives: Postcolonial film theory highlights the importance of subaltern voices and counter-narratives in challenging dominant colonial discourses. It examines how films provide platforms for marginalized and silenced voices, shedding light on the experiences and perspectives of those historically oppressed by colonialism. Postcolonial analysis explores the ways in which films contribute to the decolonization of narratives and the reclamation of agency and representation.

4. Cultural Appropriation and Orientalism: Postcolonial film theory critically examines the appropriation and exoticization of non-Western cultures by Western filmmakers. It investigates how films perpetuate orientalist tropes and stereotypes, reinforcing power imbalances and cultural hierarchies. Postcolonial analysis seeks to challenge and subvert these representations, advocating for authentic and respectful portrayals of cultural diversity.

5. Globalization and Neocolonialism: Postcolonial film theory recognizes the ways in which neocolonial power structures persist in the postcolonial era. It examines the impact of globalization, economic imperialism, and cultural hegemony on postcolonial societies. Postcolonial analysis explores the ways in which films reflect and critique these ongoing power dynamics, calling for social and political transformation.

Relevance and Contemporary Application

Postcolonial film theory remains relevant and influential in contemporary film analysis and criticism. It provides a critical lens through which scholars and critics can examine the representation of colonial and postcolonial experiences in films and the ways in which power dynamics and cultural identities are negotiated on screen.

Contemporary filmmakers often draw on postcolonial principles to create films that challenge colonial legacies, explore cultural identities, and promote social justice. They engage with postcolonial themes such as decolonization, hybridity, and the politics of representation. Postcolonial film analysis enables a deeper understanding of these creative choices, highlighting the ways in which filmmakers contribute to postcolonial discourse and engage with the complexities of colonial histories.

Moreover, postcolonial film theory's influence extends beyond traditional cinema to other forms of visual media, including documentaries, web series, and digital content. It provides a framework for analyzing the representation of postcolonial experiences in a wide range of visual narratives, examining the ways in which films contribute to the ongoing struggles for cultural, social, and political liberation.

In conclusion, postcolonial film theory offers a critical framework for analyzing the representation of colonial and postcolonial experiences in films, challenging colonial ideologies, and advocating for cultural diversity and social justice. By examining colonialism, cultural identity, subaltern voices, cultural appropriation, and neocolonialism, postcolonial film analysis provides valuable insights into the ways in which films reflect and engage with the complexities of colonial histories and the ongoing struggles for decolonization and cultural liberation. Postcolonial film theory remains relevant in contemporary film analysis, empowering scholars and critics to engage with films through a postcolonial lens and promote inclusive and transformative narratives within the cinematic landscape.

Queer Film Theory in Film Study

Queer film theory is a critical framework that examines the representation of LGBTQ+ identities and experiences in films, explores issues of sexual orientation and gender identity, and challenges heteronormative ideologies within cinematic narratives. It emerged in the late 20th century as part of the broader queer theory movement, which seeks to challenge and deconstruct normative understandings of sexuality and gender. Queer film theory aims to analyze the ways in which films portray and construct queer identities, desires, and communities, while also critiquing and subverting dominant heteronormative narratives. This essay will delve into the key concepts and principles of queer film theory, its historical development, and its relevance in contemporary film analysis.

Historical Context and Development

Queer film theory emerged in the 1990s, coinciding with the rise of queer studies and the LGBTQ+ rights movement. It drew inspiration from feminist film theory and poststructuralist theory, particularly the work of Michel Foucault and Judith Butler, to explore the representation of queer identities and desires in films. Queer film theorists sought to challenge the marginalization and misrepresentation of LGBTQ+

individuals in cinema and to interrogate the ways in which heteronormativity shapes cinematic narratives.

Key Concepts and Principles

1. Queer Representation: Queer film theory focuses on the representation of LGBTQ+ identities and experiences in films. It examines how films construct and perpetuate normative understandings of gender and sexuality and how they either challenge or reinforce dominant heteronormative narratives. Queer analysis looks for nuanced and authentic portrayals of queer characters and communities, challenging stereotypes and binary understandings of sexuality and gender.

2. Queer Spectatorship: Queer film theory considers the experiences and perspectives of queer viewers in engaging with cinematic narratives. It explores how queer spectators negotiate their identities and desires while watching films, and how they might find moments of identification or resistance within the heteronormative framework. Queer analysis highlights the importance of queer audiences in

shaping and interpreting the meanings of films.

3.   Intersectionality: Queer film theory recognizes that queerness intersects with other aspects of identity, such as race, class, and disability. It examines the ways in which multiple axes of oppression and privilege intersect with queerness and how these intersections shape the representation and experiences of LGBTQ+ individuals in films. Queer analysis emphasizes an intersectional approach that accounts for the diverse lived experiences within the queer community.

4.   Queer Subversion and Resistance: Queer film theory seeks to subvert and resist heteronormative ideologies and narratives within cinematic representations. It explores how films challenge societal norms, disrupt binary understandings of gender and sexuality, and provide alternative narratives and representations. Queer analysis examines the ways in which films can be used as tools for social critique, activism, and empowerment within the LGBTQ+ community.

5.   Queer Aesthetics: Queer film theory also explores the aesthetics and formal elements of queer cinema. It examines how filmmakers use cinematography, editing, sound, and other cinematic techniques to convey queer experiences, desires, and identities. Queer analysis considers the ways in which formal choices contribute to the queering of cinematic narratives and challenge normative aesthetics.

Relevance and Contemporary Application

Queer film theory continues to be relevant and influential in contemporary film analysis and criticism. It provides a critical lens through which scholars and critics can examine the representation of LGBTQ+ identities and experiences in films, and the ways in which cinematic narratives contribute to the broader discussions on gender and sexuality. Queer analysis allows for a more nuanced understanding of the complexities of queer representation and the impact of cinema on LGBTQ+ individuals and communities.

Contemporary filmmakers increasingly incorporate queer perspectives and principles into their work, aiming to challenge heteronormativity, address LGBTQ+ issues, and promote inclusivity. They explore themes of queer love, desire, identity, and activism, and engage with diverse queer experiences. Queer film analysis enables a deeper understanding of these creative choices, highlighting the ways in which filmmakers contribute to the queer discourse and promote social change through their storytelling.

Furthermore, queer film theory extends its influence beyond traditional cinema to other forms of visual media, including television shows, web series, and digital content. It provides a framework for analyzing the representation of LGBTQ+ identities in a wide range of visual narratives, exploring how they contribute to the visibility, acceptance, and empowerment of queer individuals.

In conclusion, queer film theory offers a critical framework for analyzing the representation of LGBTQ+ identities and experiences in films, challenging heteronormative ideologies, and advocating for inclusivity and social justice. By examining queer representation, spectatorship, intersectionality, subversion, and aesthetics, queer film analysis provides valuable insights into the ways in which films reflect and shape societal attitudes towards gender and sexuality. Queer film theory remains relevant in contemporary film analysis, empowering scholars and critics to engage with films through a queer lens and promote inclusive and transformative narratives within the cinematic landscape.

Cultural Studies Film Theory in Film Study

Cultural studies film theory is a critical framework that analyzes films within the broader context of culture, society, and power relations. It emerged in the late 20th century as an interdisciplinary field that drew from various academic disciplines, including sociology, anthropology, literary theory, and media studies. Cultural studies film theory seeks to understand how films both shape and are shaped by social, political, and cultural processes, and how they contribute to the construction of meaning and identities. This essay will explore the key concepts and principles of cultural studies film theory, its historical development, and its relevance in contemporary film analysis.

Historical Context and Development

Cultural studies emerged in the 1960s and 1970s as a response to traditional academic disciplines that focused primarily on high culture and canonical texts. It sought to challenge and deconstruct the boundaries between high and low culture, emphasizing the importance of popular culture in understanding society and identity formation. Cultural studies film theory emerged as a natural extension of this broader cultural studies approach, exploring the ways in which films function as cultural artifacts and contribute to the construction of meaning and ideology.

Key Concepts and Principles

1. Cultural Context and Meaning: Cultural studies film theory emphasizes the importance of understanding films within their cultural and historical contexts. It examines how films reflect and respond to the social, political, and cultural climate in which they are produced, and how they contribute to the production and dissemination of meaning. Cultural studies analysis explores the ways in which films engage with and influence broader cultural discourses, ideologies, and identities.

2. Popular Culture and Everyday Life: Cultural studies film theory recognizes the significance of popular culture and everyday life in shaping social and cultural dynamics. It analyzes how films reflect and represent the experiences, values, and desires of everyday people, and how they contribute to the construction of

popular imaginaries. Cultural studies analysis explores the ways in which films mediate and reflect social realities, and how they intersect with broader cultural practices and rituals.

3. Representation and Identity: Cultural studies film theory examines the representation of identities and social groups in films. It analyzes how films construct and mediate identities based on factors such as gender, race, class, sexuality, and nationality. Cultural studies analysis seeks to understand how these representations contribute to the formation of social hierarchies, stereotypes, and power relations. It also explores how audiences negotiate their own identities and meanings in relation to these representations.

4. Power and Ideology: Cultural studies film theory explores the power dynamics inherent in the production, distribution, and consumption of films. It investigates how films reflect and perpetuate dominant ideologies and discourses, and how they shape our understanding of social norms and values. Cultural studies analysis seeks to uncover the ways in which films may

reinforce or challenge existing power structures, and how they may offer alternative or oppositional readings of social reality.

5.   Reception and Audience Studies: Cultural studies film theory emphasizes the importance of audience reception and interpretation in the meaning-making process. It examines how audiences engage with films, negotiate their own meanings, and interpret them in relation to their own social and cultural contexts. Cultural studies analysis explores the ways in which audiences actively participate in the construction of meaning and the formation of cultural identities through their engagement with films.

Relevance and Contemporary Application

Cultural studies film theory remains relevant and influential in contemporary film analysis and criticism. It provides a critical framework for understanding the ways in which films both reflect and shape cultural practices, identities, and power relations. Cultural studies analysis allows scholars and critics to engage with films as cultural artifacts that are intricately connected to broader social, political, and cultural processes.

Contemporary filmmakers often draw on cultural studies principles to create films that reflect and critique social issues, challenge dominant ideologies, and engage with diverse cultural experiences. They explore themes such as globalization, hybridity, consumer culture, and the impact of media on society. Cultural studies analysis enables a deeper understanding of these creative choices, highlighting the ways in which filmmakers contribute to cultural discourses and offer alternative narratives and perspectives.

Furthermore, cultural studies film theory extends its influence beyond traditional cinema to other forms of media, including television, digital platforms, and social media. It provides a framework for analyzing the cultural significance of these media forms and their interactions with broader social and cultural dynamics.

In conclusion, cultural studies film theory offers a critical framework for analyzing films within the context of culture, society, and power relations. By examining cultural context and meaning, popular culture and everyday life, representation and identity, power and ideology, and reception and audience studies, cultural studies analysis provides valuable insights into the ways in which films shape and are shaped by broader cultural processes. Cultural studies film theory remains relevant in contemporary film analysis, empowering scholars and critics to engage with films as complex cultural artifacts and explore their significance in the construction of meaning and identities within society.

Reception Film Theory in Film Study

Reception film theory is a critical framework that focuses on the ways in which audiences receive, interpret, and engage with films. It explores the active role of viewers in the meaning-making process and emphasizes the importance of audience responses in understanding the cultural and social impact of films. Reception theory recognizes that audiences bring their own experiences, perspectives, and cultural backgrounds to the viewing process, which influences their interpretation and understanding of films. This essay will delve into the key concepts and principles of reception film theory, its historical development, and its relevance in contemporary film analysis.

Historical Context and Development
Reception film theory emerged in the 1960s and 1970s as a response to earlier film theories that predominantly focused on the analysis of films themselves, often neglecting the role of audiences. Scholars and theorists recognized that meaning is not inherent solely in the text of a film, but is constructed through the active engagement of viewers. Building upon

the foundations of reader-response theory in literary studies, reception film theory sought to understand how audiences make sense of films and how their interpretations contribute to the broader cultural discourse.

Key Concepts and Principles

1. Active Audience: Reception film theory posits that audiences are active participants in the meaning-making process. It acknowledges that viewers bring their own cultural, social, and personal backgrounds to the interpretation of films, shaping their understanding and response. The theory emphasizes that audiences are not passive recipients of meaning but actively engage with films and contribute to their interpretation and significance.

2. Encoding and Decoding: Reception film theory recognizes that filmmakers encode meaning into their films through various techniques such as narrative structure, visual aesthetics, and symbolic elements. However, it also acknowledges that audiences decode these encoded meanings based on their own cultural and social contexts.

Different viewers may interpret a film in different ways, depending on their individual experiences, values, and ideologies.

3. Interpretive Communities: Reception film theory emphasizes the existence of interpretive communities—groups of people who share similar cultural, social, or ideological backgrounds and interpret films in a similar manner. These communities provide a framework through which viewers understand and interpret films. The theory recognizes that audience interpretations are influenced by the collective norms, values, and discourses of their interpretive communities.

4. Reception Histories: Reception film theory explores the historical reception of films and how audience responses evolve over time. It acknowledges that audience interpretations can change as societal attitudes, values, and cultural contexts shift. By studying reception histories, scholars can gain insights into the evolving interpretations and cultural impact of films across different periods.

5. Active Engagement: Reception film theory emphasizes that audience engagement with films extends beyond the viewing experience. It recognizes that viewers engage in discussions, debates, and cultural practices related to films, contributing to the ongoing dialogue and cultural significance of cinematic works. The theory emphasizes the active participation of audiences in shaping the cultural reception and interpretation of films.

Relevance and Contemporary Application

Reception film theory continues to be relevant and influential in contemporary film analysis and criticism. It provides a critical lens through which scholars and critics can understand the dynamic relationship between films and audiences. By examining the active role of viewers in the meaning-making process, reception analysis allows for a more nuanced understanding of the cultural, social, and ideological impact of films.

Contemporary filmmakers often consider audience reception and engage with the principles of reception theory in their creative choices. They may intentionally leave aspects of their films open to interpretation, allowing audiences to actively engage with the narrative and contribute their own meanings. Filmmakers may also consider the diversity of audiences and aim to create works that resonate with different interpretive communities, fostering dialogue and a multiplicity of perspectives.

Reception theory is particularly relevant in the digital age, where audiences have expanded platforms for engagement and interaction. Social media platforms, online forums, and video-sharing sites enable audiences to discuss, analyze, and share their interpretations of films. This online engagement further shapes the reception of films and contributes to the ongoing dialogue surrounding cinematic works.

In conclusion, reception film theory offers a valuable framework for analyzing the ways in which audiences receive, interpret, and engage with films. By recognizing the active role of viewers, the theory emphasizes the importance of audience responses in the meaning-making process and the cultural impact of films. Reception film theory remains relevant in contemporary film analysis, empowering scholars, critics, and filmmakers to understand the dynamic relationship between films and audiences and to appreciate the diversity of interpretations and cultural significance that films can generate.

Cognitive Film Theory in Film Study

Cognitive film theory is a theoretical framework that focuses on the cognitive processes involved in the comprehension, interpretation, and appreciation of films. It draws upon cognitive psychology and cognitive science to explore how viewers perceive, process, and make meaning of cinematic works. Cognitive film theory examines the ways in which films engage with viewers' cognitive faculties, such as attention, memory, perception, and problem-solving, to create narrative comprehension and emotional responses. This essay will delve into the key concepts and principles of cognitive film theory, its historical development, and its relevance in contemporary film analysis.

Historical Context and Development

Cognitive film theory emerged in the 1980s and 1990s as an interdisciplinary approach that combined insights from cognitive psychology, linguistics, philosophy of mind, and film studies. It developed as a response to earlier film theories that primarily focused on the formal aspects of films or the social and cultural contexts in which they were produced. Cognitive film theory sought to understand the cognitive processes underlying film perception and comprehension, aiming to uncover the mechanisms by which viewers make sense of cinematic narratives.

Key Concepts and Principles

1. Perception and Attention: Cognitive film theory emphasizes the role of perception and attention in the viewing experience. It examines how viewers selectively attend to specific visual and auditory elements in the film and how their perceptual processes shape their interpretation and understanding of the narrative. The theory explores how filmmakers use visual and auditory cues to guide viewers' attention and create meaning within the film.

2. Narrative Comprehension: Cognitive film theory focuses on the cognitive processes involved in narrative comprehension. It explores how viewers extract, organize, and integrate

information from the film to construct a coherent narrative structure. The theory investigates the ways in which viewers identify characters, follow the plot, make inferences, and anticipate future events based on their cognitive schema and prior knowledge.

3. Emotion and Affect: Cognitive film theory examines how films elicit emotional and affective responses in viewers. It explores the cognitive mechanisms underlying the experience of emotions, such as empathy, suspense, and identification with characters. The theory investigates how filmmakers use narrative techniques, audiovisual elements, and storytelling strategies to evoke specific emotional responses and engage viewers' cognitive and affective processes.

4. Memory and Recall: Cognitive film theory acknowledges the role of memory in the viewing and interpretation of films. It explores how viewers encode, store, and retrieve information from the film, and how memory processes contribute to the construction of meaning. The theory investigates how filmmakers employ

narrative devices, repetition, and visual motifs to enhance memory retention and facilitate viewers' recall of important narrative elements.

5.   Problem-Solving and Cognitive Engagement: Cognitive film theory recognizes the cognitive engagement and problem-solving processes that viewers undergo while watching a film. It examines how viewers actively engage with the narrative, anticipate outcomes, and form hypotheses about the unfolding events. The theory explores how filmmakers structure narratives and create narrative gaps to engage viewers' cognitive faculties and foster a sense of involvement and intellectual stimulation.

Relevance and Contemporary Application

Cognitive film theory continues to be influential and relevant in contemporary film analysis and criticism. It provides a valuable framework for understanding the cognitive processes involved in film perception, comprehension, and emotional engagement. By examining perception, attention, narrative comprehension, emotion, memory, and problem-solving, cognitive film analysis offers insights into the ways in which films engage viewers' cognitive faculties and create meaningful and impactful viewing experiences.

Contemporary filmmakers often employ cognitive strategies and techniques in their creative choices. They may utilize visual and auditory cues to guide viewers' attention, employ narrative structures that facilitate comprehension, and elicit emotional responses through carefully crafted storytelling and audiovisual elements. Filmmakers may also experiment with narrative gaps, ambiguities, and complex narratives to engage viewers' cognitive processes and encourage active interpretation and engagement.

In the digital age, cognitive film theory intersects with studies on interactive and immersive media, virtual reality, and augmented reality. Scholars and researchers explore the cognitive aspects of these technologies and their potential impact on the viewing experience. They investigate how these technologies can shape attention, perception, memory, and emotion in ways distinct from traditional cinema, opening up new avenues for cognitive film analysis.

In conclusion, cognitive film theory provides a valuable framework for understanding the cognitive processes involved in the perception, comprehension, and emotional engagement of films. By examining perception, attention, narrative comprehension, emotion, memory, and problem-solving, cognitive film analysis sheds light on the ways in which films engage viewers' cognitive faculties and create meaningful viewing experiences. Cognitive film theory remains relevant in contemporary film analysis, offering insights into the ways filmmakers can optimize the cognitive impact of their works and exploring the intersection between cinema and cognitive psychology.

Ecocriticism Film Theory in Film Study

Ecocriticism film theory is a critical framework that examines the intersection of film and the natural environment. It explores how films represent, engage with, and comment on ecological issues, such as environmental degradation, climate change, and the human-nature relationship. Ecocriticism film theory draws from the field of ecocriticism, which emerged in the late 20th century as a response to the environmental crisis and the need for literary and cultural analysis of nature and the environment. This essay will explore the key concepts and principles of ecocriticism film theory, its historical development, and its relevance in contemporary film analysis.

Historical Context and Development
Ecocriticism film theory emerged in the late 20th century alongside the broader ecocriticism movement. It developed in

response to the growing awareness of environmental issues and the need for critical engagement with the representation of nature in literature, art, and popular culture. Ecocritics recognized the power of film as a medium to shape perceptions of the natural world and to engage audiences in environmental discourse. Ecocriticism film theory builds upon the foundations of ecocriticism, extending its focus to the analysis of film as a cultural artifact.

Key Concepts and Principles

1. Nature Representation: Ecocriticism film theory examines how films represent nature and the natural environment. It explores the ways in which filmmakers depict landscapes, ecosystems, animals, and plants, and how these representations contribute to the construction of environmental narratives and meanings. The theory investigates how filmmakers use visual aesthetics, narrative techniques, and storytelling strategies to convey ecological themes and messages.

2. Human-Nature Relationship: Ecocriticism film theory explores the complex relationship between humans

and the natural world as depicted in films. It investigates how films portray human interactions with nature, including the exploitation of natural resources, environmental activism, and the consequences of human actions on the environment. The theory examines the ways in which films represent the interconnectedness and interdependence of humans and the natural world.

3. Environmental Ethics: Ecocriticism film theory engages with environmental ethics and the moral implications of human interactions with the natural environment. It explores how films raise ethical questions and dilemmas related to environmental issues, such as the responsibility of individuals and societies towards nature, environmental justice, and sustainable living. The theory examines how filmmakers use storytelling and character development to explore these ethical dimensions.

4. Eco-Aesthetics: Ecocriticism film theory recognizes the importance of visual aesthetics in the representation of nature in films. It explores how

filmmakers use cinematography, lighting, color, and sound to evoke emotional responses and create a sense of environmental presence. The theory investigates how eco-aesthetics can enhance viewers' connections with the natural world, fostering empathy and environmental consciousness.

5. Activism and Advocacy: Ecocriticism film theory acknowledges the potential of films to inspire environmental activism and advocacy. It examines how films can raise awareness, mobilize audiences, and contribute to environmental discourse and social change. The theory investigates the ways in which films can act as a platform for environmental activism, promoting sustainability, conservation, and environmental justice.

Relevance and Contemporary Application

Ecocriticism film theory remains relevant and influential in contemporary film analysis and criticism, particularly in light of the global environmental challenges we face. It provides a critical framework for understanding the representation of nature and ecological issues in films and for analyzing their impact on audience perceptions and attitudes towards the environment.

Contemporary filmmakers increasingly engage with ecocriticism principles in their creative choices. They may create films that focus explicitly on environmental themes, incorporating scientific knowledge, ecological storytelling, and environmental activism. Filmmakers may also employ innovative cinematic techniques to immerse viewers in the natural world, emphasizing the beauty, fragility, and interconnectedness of ecosystems.

In the age of digital media and online streaming platforms, ecocriticism film theory extends its reach to include the analysis of nature documentaries, environmental web series, and online campaigns that promote ecological awareness. It explores the potential of new media to engage audiences in environmental discourse and foster a sense of ecological responsibility.

In conclusion, ecocriticism film theory offers a valuable framework for analyzing the representation of nature, ecological themes, and environmental ethics in films. By examining nature representation, the human-nature relationship, environmental ethics, eco-aesthetics, and activism, ecocriticism film analysis contributes to our understanding of how films shape our perceptions of the natural world and our engagement with environmental issues. Ecocriticism film theory remains relevant and timely, highlighting the potential of cinema to raise environmental awareness, inspire activism, and contribute to the broader environmental discourse.

Social, emotional, psychological theory (SEP) Film Theory

The social, emotional, psychological theory of film studies explores the ways in which films influence and interact with individuals and society on a social, emotional, and psychological level. This theory recognizes that films have the power to shape our perceptions, beliefs, and emotions and that they can serve as a reflection and commentary on social and psychological issues.

Here are the key components of this theory:

1. Social Impact: Films can have a profound impact on society by depicting social issues, cultural values, and historical events. They can raise awareness, challenge social norms, and inspire social change. For example, films

like "12 Years a Slave" or "Schindler's List" shed light on historical injustices and promote empathy and understanding.

2.   Emotional Engagement: Films have the ability to evoke a wide range of emotions in viewers. Through storytelling, character development, and audiovisual techniques, films can make us laugh, cry, and feel fear, joy, or anger. Emotional engagement is crucial for our attachment to the characters and the narrative, allowing us to connect with the film's themes and messages.

3.   Psychological Impact: Films can explore and delve into various psychological aspects of the human experience. They can depict complex characters, delve into the human psyche, and explore psychological themes such as identity, memory, trauma, or mental health. Psychological theories and concepts can be applied to analyze characters and understand their motivations and behaviours.

4.   Audience Reception: The theory also emphasizes the role of the audience in interpreting and engaging with films. Each viewer brings their own

background, experiences, and beliefs, which shape their understanding and emotional response to the film. Audience reception theory examines how films are received and interpreted by different individuals or groups, considering factors such as culture, gender, age, and personal experiences.

5.   Catharsis and Escapism: Films can provide both cathartic and escapist experiences for viewers. Catharsis refers to the emotional release or purification that occurs through identifying with the characters' experiences and resolving conflicts on screen. Escapism, on the other hand, allows viewers to temporarily disconnect from reality and immerse themselves in fictional worlds, offering entertainment and temporary relief from everyday life.

By studying films through the lens of social, emotional, psychological theory, film scholars and analysts can gain a deeper understanding of the impact and influence of cinema on individuals and society. This approach allows for critical analysis, interpretation, and discussion of the complex ways in which films shape our thoughts, emotions, and social perceptions.